Kansas Wetlands
A Wildlife Treasury

Kansas Wetlands
A Wildlife Treasury

Joseph T. Collins   Suzanne L. Collins   Bob Gress

Foreword by John E. Hayes, Jr., Western Resources, and
Jim Minnerath, U.S. Fish and Wildlife Service

With photographs by   David Birmingham   Mike Blair
Suzanne L. Collins   Bob Gress   Steve Mulligan
Garold Sneegas   Gerald J. Wiens

Publication made possible in part by Western Resources

University Press of Kansas

Published by the University Press of Kansas
(Lawrence, Kansas 66049), which was organized by the
Kansas Board of Regents and is operated and funded by
Emporia State University, Fort Hays State University,
Kansas State University, Pittsburg State University, the
University of Kansas, and Wichita State University

Photographs on pages 1, 2, 4–5, 8, 10, and endleaves
by Bob Gress
This book is printed on acid-free paper.

Library of Congress Cataloging-in-Publication Data

Collins, Joseph T.
Kansas wetlands: a wildlife treasury / Joseph T. Collins,
Suzanne L. Collins, Bob Gress ; foreword by John E.
Hayes, Jr., and Jim Minnerath ; with photographs by
David Birmingham ...[et al.].
p. cm.
Includes bibliographical references and index.
ISBN 0-7006-0635-1 (cloth)
1. Wetland fauna—Kansas—Pictorial works. 2. Wet-
lands—Kansas—Pictorial works. I. Collins, Suzanne L.
II. Gress, Bob. III. Title.
QL177.C64 1994
591.781—dc20   94-18368

Printed in Hong Kong   10 9 8 7 6 5 4 3 2 1

I dedicate this book to my friend, Thomas J. Sloan, whose support and encouragement of my endeavors has been so vital. Because of his efforts, Kansas and its people are better informed about their natural environment and the need to protect it in the coming millennium. He is also an accomplished sheep rancher.   *Joseph T. Collins*

In memory of Jane Topping Combest. Wendy's wonder of nature awakened the best in all who knew her.   *Suzanne L. Collins*

I dedicate this book to my parents, Bert and Nina Mae Gress, who taught me to love and appreciate the natural world.   *Bob Gress*

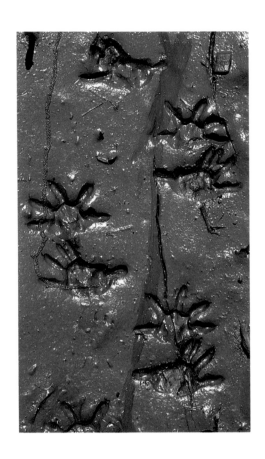

Contents

Foreword

AT LONG LAST, three leading Kansas naturalists set into print praise for the unheralded smaller wetlands that ephemerally and resiliently enrich the landscape of our state. In an age when wetlands are being destroyed through ignorance, it is crucial to promote understanding of their wonderfully diverse and dynamic nature. As Leigh Frederickson once said, "Our seasonal wetlands are like Christmas tree lights twinkling across the North American continent, some twinkle longer and more often than others, yet all are vital to the system."

Joseph T. Collins, Suzanne L. Collins, and Bob Gress have done a delightful job of revealing the virtues of these forgotten wetlands. Briefly, and sometimes humorously, they describe the lives of creatures that depend on the wet-dry-wet cycle of temporary waters, a rhythm found nowhere else in nature's scheme. Their color photographs capture the immense variety of wetlands wildlife that exists so close to our homes.

Every Kansan has a role to play in protecting wetlands. Western Resources and the U.S. Fish and Wildlife Service take great pleasure in sponsoring this book. We believe that such a cooperative venture between private enterprise and government bodes well for the future of Kansas wetlands. We are committed to protecting all living things, and we believe the 127 photographs in this volume provide eloquent testimony why you should be, too. Without wetlands, we would all be poorer and less aware of the diversity that the earth can produce and that we, as environmental stewards, must protect for the future.

John E. Hayes, Jr.
Chairman of the Board, President,
and Chief Executive Officer
Western Resources

Jim Minnerath
Flint Hills National Wildlife Refuge
U.S. Fish and Wildlife Service
Department of the Interior

Sights, sounds and smells for the human senses.
Challenges for the human mind.
Something for the human spirit.
Wet and secret home of wildlife.
Wetlands
Jewels in the necklace of the Earth.   *Dan Kilby, Wichita Audubon Society*

Preface

THIS IS A BOOK about the wildlife of Kansas wetlands, featuring photographs by seven naturalists taken over the last thirty-five years. All of the portraits in this book were made from color slides. The photographers featured here have spent enormous amounts of time traveling to Kansas wetlands in order to locate, learn about, and photograph the creatures shown on the following pages. They visited every major wetland in the state and spent a lot of time in these damp situations, enduring the sucking mud and treacherous stumps in oxbows and swamps and the hidden snags and sinkholes that make wading in these shallow jewels while carrying a camera such an exciting pastime.

During the years of studying wetlands creatures and photographing them, we have become indebted to many people and organizations for help, courtesies, and kindnesses. These include Binion Amerson, Pat Anderson, Ray E. Ashton, Gene Bahr, Jerry Bailey, Roger Boyd, Mary Butel, Janalee P. Caldwell, Martin B. Capron, Robert F. Clarke, Ken Davidson, Mary E. Dawson, David M. Dennis, Michael Ehlebracht, Connie Elpers, Ruth D. Fauhl, Gary W. Ferguson, Nancy Green, Bill Gress, David Grow, Hank Guarisco, Karen Hamrick, Cheryl Harrod, Connie Hay, Scott Hillard, Dave Hilley, Judy Hills, Corson Hirschfeld, Wayne Hoffman, Marilyn Holley, Philip S. Humphrey, Juanita M. Hunter, David Huyser, Kelly J. Irwin, Jeannette Johnson, Eric Juterbock, Milan Kiminiak, Richard Lattis, Charlotte Leviton, Raymond Loraine, David Lucas, Tim Martz, Jim Mason, Delfi Messinger, Larry Miller, Jim Minnerath, Victor Moss, Chris Parsons, Janice Perry, Marjorie Perry, George R. Pisani, George Potts, Bill Pracht, Jim Pritchard, Stanley Roth, Terry D. Schwaner, Marvin Schwilling, Shelly Skie, Gail Sloan, Dean Steiner, Robert Sudlow, Richard Sugarman, Charles Swank, John Tollefson, Gail Underwood, Gary Wallace, Chelsea R. Weaver, Nancy K. Weaver, Dick Whelan, Jeffrey Whipple, Bernard Willard, Eva Williams, Stan Wood, the Natural History Museum and School of Education, the University of Kansas, the Kansas Herpetological Society, the Wichita Audubon Society, and the Wichita Department of Parks and Recreation. We also take great pleasure in thanking Dan Kilby for the use of his poem.

Rex C. Buchanan, Craig C. Freeman, and John L. Zimmerman read the text for this book and made numerous helpful suggestions. We are indebted to them for their insights and ideas. Any errors remain ours alone.

Joseph T. Collins
Suzanne L. Collins
Bob Gress

29 January 1994

Kansas Wetlands: A Different Perspective

WATER IS GOOD, praised Lao-tzu, the founder of Taoism. "It benefits all things and does not compete with them. It dwells in places that all disdain." People disdain those places, as this book makes clear by image and word, at their own peril. Much of value in the natural world depends upon those lowly places, wetlands, where land and water marry. Without wetlands, the biodiversity of the world, and Kansas, would suffer. As James Lovelock reminds us, "We are wrong . . . to preserve just orchids and cuddly animals; what needs saving are the habitats that nurtured them. . . . We cherish the rare, for they signify a healthy world. We judge habitats by their tolerance for eccentrics. Today's oddities may include a future commonplace needed to cope with tomorrow's world."

The wetlands of Kansas nurture a treasury of both eccentric and commonplace creatures. By any measure, the diversity of wildlife in or near the approximately one percent of Kansas acreage that is wetlands greatly exceeds that of the dry ninety-nine percent, including the Flint Hills prairies, High Plains desert-grasslands, rugged Red Hills canyons, and even the relatively moist eastern forests of the Osage Cuestas. Water is the life-giving element that lures animals into all these normally dry habitats, and it is in and around these ephemeral waterways that the greatest numbers and kinds of wildlife are to be found. The species lists in John Zimmerman's fine book, *Cheyenne Bottoms: Wetlands in Jeopardy* (1990, University Press of Kansas) attest to this abundance—9 amphibians, 18 reptiles, 324 birds, and 20 mammals, for a total of 371 kinds of semi-aquatic or terrestrial animals living in and around that vast inland marsh alone. Put another way, Cheyenne Bottoms is home, permanently or seasonally, to slightly more than sixty percent of the 610 known vertebrate species (excluding fishes) found in Kansas, and this variety must certainly hold true for virtually all of the larger freshwater wetlands of the state, such as the Marais des Cygnes and Neosho Wildlife Areas in the east. To the west, the larger sinks like Big Basin and Little Basin and the many other scattered playa basins probably support fewer plants and animals, but these wetlands are even more precious to those creatures that depend upon them. Rainfall on the western plains is usually brief and sparse, and wildlife keeps a constant awareness of those places that hold water, however temporarily. Given the abundance and diversity of animals around wetlands, great and small, west or east, such areas are the best places to see wildlife in our state.

Wetlands are transition areas that lie between terrestrial and aquatic ecosystems. Owing to their position in a habitat, mainly between dry uplands and low permanent water, wetlands intercept rainstorm runoff from the higher ground before it reaches lower places of deep water. Situated as they are, wetlands act as a natural filter, slowing rainwater velocity and trapping silts and sediments that flow through them, thus helping maintain and improve the water quality in lakes, streams, and rivers. Today, these trapped silts and sediments contain pesticides and other harmful pollutants and toxins, so the role of wetlands in cleansing the water has become even more vital to wildlife and people. Unfortunately, wetlands themselves have become more degraded. Nonetheless, they continue to protect wildlife and people while struggling to survive against ever-growing pressures of human culture. From a wildlife standpoint, small transitory waters are the only true wetlands, the kind that experience a recurring dry phase of varying duration. Permanent lakes, ponds, and streams can go dry also, but the difference between them and wetlands is that wildlife living in permanent water is wiped out in dry times because it is not adapted to survive them. Creatures that live in wetlands are adapted to the cycle of dry-wet-dry-wet and do remarkably well while less fortunate kin, owing their existence to permanent water, suffer the consequences of inflexibility in their habitat requirements. Only certain kinds of creatures can make it in a true wetlands, but those that can are well adapted for them.

Some famous Kansas wetlands, like Cheyenne Bottoms or Quivira National Wildlife Refuge, are seasonally spectacular, sporting a gaudy, raucous birdlife in numbers that can numb the senses during spring and fall migrations. Even in winter, these same wetlands retain a frigid majesty as cold winter winds roar across their vast waters and mudflats. Mention wetlands in Kansas, and most people think only of these well-publicized, high-profile places. Because of their exposure in the media, these celebrated and impressive marshes are mistakenly regarded as typical Kansas wetlands. But typical they are not. Only a handful of Kansas wetlands can boast of broad expanses of shallow water with profuse aquatic vegetation and thousands of birds. Most of them are much smaller, temporary habitats, unimpressive visually and easily overlooked. Many are damaged or drained and filled with rock, then flattened and covered with concrete. Others are leveled and plowed to grow crops. These little ones are the forgotten, neglected wetlands of Kansas.

They are wetlands that don't fit the preconceived notion with respect to expanse of water and hardpan or large numbers of migratory birds. Often dry during times of normal rainfall, they are places that gather runoff from winter thaw, mix in the rain of spring to make a fresh and fertile soup, and then are burned dry by the heat of summer sun until they disappear. Temporarily they become low places of wet potency, parched canals and depressions patiently awaiting the next winter rainfall so that the cycle can begin anew. These little wetlands, though unsung, outnumber by the thousands the big marshes in Kansas—like the Neosho and Marais des Cygnes Wildlife Areas, the Jamestown Marsh, or the McPherson Wetlands. Though they receive little attention from us and even less respect, they constitute the most fundamental of all wildlife habitats in our state. Without them, much of our wildlife would disappear forever.

These diminutive wetlands include woodland floodpools. Dark and humid, a flooded woodland in eastern Kansas seems a prehistoric environment, a silent place of still water shaded by Cottonwood, Green Ash, and Hackberry. Beams of sun pierce the canopy and highlight branches and stumps where Black-winged Damselflies flit and sit. It is a place where salamanders cavort in the unlit shallows, carrying on their intricate amphibian courtship. Most frogs like the brisk cold and enter woodland pools early, during the rains of February. Later, the warmth-loving Gray Treefrogs weigh in with their June chorus. Wood Ducks nest and raise their young near these woodland ponds, and Raccoons wade in them, their paws constantly searching for a tasty morsel. White-tailed Deer, ever wary and hard to see, slip silently through the forest and stop to drink, tails twitching and big ears alert for the slightest noise. Woodland floodpools are wetlands. Ancient wetlands.

Among these small wetlands are roadside ditches. Roadside ditches are everywhere. We make them when we borrow the surrounding dirt to construct an uplifted earthen platform for a gravel or asphalt roadway, leaving a ditch on each side of the route. After a few years, if left to seed and untreated by pesticides and herbicides, such a ditch undergoes a vital transformation. Cattails emerge. Smartweed is present. During late winter in eastern Kansas, after the first cold rain has heralded the coming of spring, Smallmouth Salamanders crawl under cover of darkness to the ditch and begin their courtship ritual. Almost simultaneously, male frogs of many kinds congregate at the ditch to sing, eagerly awaiting the arrival of the females. As spring progresses, the males of such amphibian species as Narrowmouth Toads show up, hide in the emerging vegetation, and soon begin their bleating call, sounding just like a flock of sheep. Crayfishes appear in the ditch, and when summer arrives, Crayfish Snakes can be found along the edge of the roadside ditch, hunting them for dinner.

Out in western Kansas, roadside ditches assume more significance for wildlife because rainfall is so elusive and must be captured and held for a little while so creatures can make brief but important use of it. Chances of a late winter rain in the west are unpredictable. In fact it may not rain until July, and it may not rain at all during any given season. So amphibians out west must be alert and aware of their opportunities to breed and ensure the survival of their kind. As the great rainstorms surge eastward over the Rockies and are sucked nearly dry, as the winds roar down across the plains of western Kansas and drop their remaining moisture, the frogs take what is left. Roadside ditches catch the meager offering and hold it just long enough for frog eggs to be laid and to hatch. The tadpoles frantically eat, grow, and metamorphose into miniature adults in a race against the merciless, dehydrating sun that threatens to evaporate the water from the ditch upon which their very existence depends. In western Kansas, these small wetlands may see this cycle repeated many times in the course of a season; or a year or two may pass before the ditches fill once more and toads lustily sing and breed. Roadside ditches are wetlands. Elementary wetlands.

The shallow marsh of an oxbow is a miniature wetland. Oxbows are made as a river changes course, shifting and twisting and bending like a reptile, leaving behind a bow-shaped pool isolated from the main channel and abandoned to the forces of nature—rain, cold, and heat. No longer flowing, they become tranquil and flush with Buttonbushes and Bulrushes. Black Willows line their edges. Bullfrogs breed in them, as do Snapping Turtles and Yellow Mud Turtles. Water Striders glide and skitter across the surface in every direction, looking for dinner and dodging those who would dine on them. Water Snakes swim gracefully into the shallows at night in search of frogs for dinner. Kingfishers and Great Blue Herons are the daytime hunters, making a meal from fishes and crayfishes trapped when the river disowned the oxbow and forced it to the sideline. Prairie Cordgrasses and Spikerushes appear, while Dolomedes Spiders fish for their prey along the water's edge. Red-winged Blackbirds sing and establish territories. Rough Green Snakes balance gracefully and motionlessly in the green bushes along the shore, impossible to detect unless they lunge for a tasty insect. Muskrats make their home in these places. Double-crested Cormorants perch on nearby logs and branches where they spread their wings in the sun to dry. Oxbows are wetlands. Primal wetlands.

Wet meadows are small, overlooked wetlands. Wet meadows crop up on lowland prairies that don't drain well and remain saturated for most of the year. Foxtail, Prairie Cordgrass, Eastern Gamagrass, and Sedges abound on these moist level meadows. Crayfishes build their mounds on them, little lumpy spires with an opening at the top; Crawfish Frogs sometimes take possession of a mound and build a platform at the side where they emerge and sit of an evening, taking the air and an occasional insect for dinner. All kinds of frogs and toads love these meadows and live there the entire year. Any concentration of such amphibians is bound to attract a hungry Ribbon Snake or Garter Snake. Killdeer, Common Snipe, and Pectoral Sandpipers roam these spongy meadows, snapping up unwary insects. Massasaugas, those snappy, venomous little rattlesnakes so plentiful at Cheyenne Bottoms, find wet meadows a favorable habitat for a variety of small rodents that make a good snake meal. Wet meadows are wetlands. Vigorous wetlands.

Railroad ditches are the oldest ditch habitat in Kansas, east or west. Whether active or abandoned, the watery ditches that border these elevated steel ribbons still feature many of the native plants and animals that were settled in Kansas long before the trains arrived. They are narrow but important glimpses of a natural heritage that once dominated the state. Green-backed Herons still silently stalk the edges of these century-old places, while Common Snipe stay hidden in the bordering vegetation. Within a few feet of the watery ditch, Broadhead Skinks find abandoned railroad ties lying on the slopes below the tracks and think them excellent places to lay their eggs and bring forth their young, brightly striped with yellow on black, all of it giving way to a brilliant blue tail that is the envy of other lizards. Plainbelly Water Snakes spend much time here too, searching for frogs to eat and basking on the fallen limbs and logs that clog the canal-like ditch. Railroad ditches are wetlands. Vital wetlands.

Backyard rainpools are ephemeral, unsung wetlands. Rainpools are the smallest and most basic wetland in the world. Although we ignore them, nearly every other living creature uses them, from drinking deer to frolicking frog. At one time, Cheyenne Bottoms, the huge wetlands in central Kansas, was the biggest backyard rainpool in the state. But it fluctuated a bit too much, so dikes were installed to control the water and make sure it was there when the ducks, geese, and shorebirds needed it. Now it is world famous, the crucial stopover for migrating birds in the central flyway of North America. It is also mecca to the local reptiles and myriad amphibians. While Cheyenne Bottoms commands our respect and concern, small backyard rainpools go unsung. But small amphibians recognize their vitality. Salamanders, frogs, and toads are not about to undertake long hikes to reach the Bottoms when a fresh rainpool is close by, just right for breeding. While backyard rainpools are a source of drinking water for many small birds, reptiles, and mammals, amphibians are the primary inhabitants of small wetlands worldwide and use them at a more elemental level—as prime breeding sites. Backyard rainpools are wetlands. Fertile wetlands.

Of course not all wetlands are ignored, and this book gives ample attention to the big marshes in Kansas. For year-round enjoyment, visit Quivira, Jamestown, or Cheyenne Bottoms. Take a trip to the Neosho or Marais des Cygnes Wildlife Areas. Hop in the car and cruise out to Big Basin. Tote along some of the books we recommend in the "Suggested Reading." Be prepared to see a lot of wildlife. And when you do, use your imagination. Think of what these wetlands were like before European settlement, when Native Americans saw them abrim with vitality.

When European settlers arrived, it is estimated that the continental United States was covered from sea to shining sea with 220 million acres of wetlands. Today, less than half remains. At the beginning of settlement, some precursor to a modern-day developer hung the moniker "wastelands" on them, and it stuck. In the succeeding decades, pressures to drain any and all low, wet places grew stronger and stronger. Consistently undervalued, wetlands have succumbed to the efforts to turn them into drier, higher ground to make way for development and agriculture. In the 1980s even the federal government threatened wetlands when it tried to narrow their definition, thus removing many areas from regulatory protection. A 1991 series of articles published by the *Kansas City Star* found, for example, that the Department of Agriculture allowed U.S. farmers to drain 185,000 acres of wetlands contrary to a 1985 congressional directive.

Recently there have been some hopeful signs for wetlands, particularly the larger ones. The federal government has dropped its ill-advised efforts to bring more wetlands under the plow. At the local level in Kansas, an urban site, the Pracht Wetland, is being promoted for the educational opportunities it can provide in the Wichita area. Statewide, the Kansas Department of Wildlife and Parks has begun to acquire some of the more important wetland breeding sites for endangered or threatened amphibians.

In a recent series of articles for the Kansas Chapter of the Nature Conservancy, Craig Freeman of the Kansas Biological Survey had this to say about Kansas wetlands: "Water quality and water quantity are key factors affecting life in the Great

Plains. Wetlands occupied less than two percent of the state's nearly 53 million acres in the late 1700s, and nearly half of these may since have been lost. Nevertheless, wetland natural communities provide sanctuary for much of the state's biota." He goes on to point out that "over three-fourths of the threatened and endangered species in Kansas inhabit or depend on wetlands or aquatic habitats." A recent publication issued by the Kansas Department of Wildlife and Parks, *Wetland and Riparian Areas of Kansas: Resources in Need of Conservation*, stated that the specific loss of wetlands in the state since the 1780s was about 405,000 acres. The report showed that 28,766 wetland acres in Kansas were currently owned or controlled directly by the state or federal government. In other words, around the late 1700s, there were about 848,000 acres of wetlands in Kansas, and almost half of them were drained or filled by the 1980s. That's pretty depressing. Even more disturbing, to date only about seven percent of those designated wetland acres have been permanently acquired or are controlled by the state or federal government, and those acres are listed as being part of thirty-two larger refuges or parks. These numbers suggest that we need to set aside a lot more of our wetlands, preferably in a cooperative effort by corporations, private organizations, and government that can come up with a long-range plan for the future of wetlands wildlife in our state. However difficult, the enduring value of wetlands, for both wildlife and people makes the effort seem mandatory.

It may take a real effort to appreciate these small, cryptic wetlands. They are often seasonally dry and dull, and thus can be enjoyed only when rainfall renews them and they spring back to life. But their impact on Kansas wildlife is greater than that of any other habitat in our state. They are everywhere within casual walking distance. After the next heavy rain, take a stroll through the suburbs of your town. You will easily find a backyard rainpool or roadside ditch, and if you are walking at night, it will probably be brimming with creatures. Hike further out of town and veer over to the nearest grove of trees sitting on a floodplain or other lowland. There you will probably discover a woodland pool, and may hear the "ker plunk" of a startled frog diving for safety. Or take a trail down by the railroad tracks and check out the water-filled sloughs teeming with wildlife. Or walk along the edge of your local river or stream and discover the oxbows and low spots filled with quiet, temporary water and animals and plants. The diversity and numbers of wildlife that count on these temporary waters makes them a glittering achievement of the Kansas landscape. They are small glistening gems scattered across our prairies and forests, sparkling spots in our suburbs and villages, all spread out like moist way stations. They are stepping stones between the big wetlands that lead in no single direction, but interconnect the Marais des Cygnes Refuge with Cheyenne Bottoms and it with Big Basin, forming a mosaic of little wet places—jewels in the wilderness necklace of our Kansas environment. We must be careful not to break the delicate strand.

The nesting Snowy Egret shown here is displaying its ornate nuptial plumes, called aigrettes. In the late 1800s, great numbers of these birds were slaughtered so the feathers could be used to adorn ladies' hats. At that time, the entire population of the Snowy Egret dropped so low that the birds have become a regular wetland sight only within the last ten years. In Kansas, they breed in nesting colonies along with other species of herons. Sometimes the colonies are located in the tops of large Cattail clumps; at other times they may nest in trees miles from the closest water. Photograph by Bob Gress.

The original population of Kansas River Otters disappeared in 1904 when the last animal was found near Manhattan. After being reintroduced in the state, these active, inquisitive creatures have recently been observed on the Neosho River and its wetland backwaters at the Flint Hills National Wildlife Refuge. Graceful and powerful swimmers, they are entertaining to watch. A River Otter is the envy of most anglers, because it is capable of outmaneuvering and capturing even the fastest of fish. These semi-aquatic mammals are bigger than most people realize—adults may be four feet long and weigh up to twenty-five pounds. Photograph by Bob Gress.

White-tailed Deer are among our largest wild mammals and are found in all kinds of habitats, ranging from dry wooded uplands to lush wetlands. The abundance of succulent plant life make wetlands ideal feeding areas for these creatures. Deer are normally seen foraging at dawn and dusk. When startled, they can run surprisingly fast through wetland shallows. As they run, they raise their tail, "flagging" it from side to side. Fleeing White-tailed Deer can easily stay together as they follow the flag in front of them. When they stop, the tail drops and they appear to instantly vanish because they blend so well with the surroundings. After feeding at wetlands, White-tails may return to bordering woodlands or lie down in lowland areas with tall cover, where they spend the day chewing their cuds and resting. Photograph by David Birmingham.

Bite, bite, bite. Like most aquatic serpents of its ilk, the Northern Water Snake is a behavioral broken record when bothered. These watchful, wetland-loving reptiles keep their distance from people, but when cornered or grabbed, they give as good as they get. Northerns have the widest range of any water snake in Kansas and therefore offer the greatest opportunity for a human-snake encounter, along with the attendant excitement. Photograph by Suzanne L. Collins.

Crawdads get very nervous when the Graham's Crayfish Snake steps out, so to speak, for a night of hunting along roadside ditches in eastern Kansas. The Graham's feeds exclusively on crawdads, no matter how they are caught and prepared (or caught unprepared). Unlike its cousins, the water snakes, this reptile is relatively shy and retiring, displaying little of the aggressive behavior for which water snakes are notorious. In fact, because of its unassuming nature, few people are aware that this serpent lives in their neighborhood wetlands. Photograph by Suzanne L. Collins.

The Checkered Garter Snake loves wet places. Unfortunately, it lives down along the Oklahoma border, in the Red Hills and southern High Plains where water is a precious commodity. Here it ekes out an existence hunting toads, lizards, mice, and insects and endures a mostly dry, hot climate. After a thunderstorm, though, life is good for this reptile. Prey becomes abundant, and the snake grows fat and has babies, and once again the lineage of these slender fellows is preserved, all because rain fell and made wetlands—again. Photograph by Suzanne L. Collins.

When a few birds discover a hot fishing spot, others notice, and before long it's birds wing to wing, and the fish appear to be outnumbered. Disputes arise, beaks jab, and feuds begin and end and begin again. This avian fishing hole is located at Quivira National Wildlife Refuge in central Kansas. Most of these birds are Snowy Egrets, with some Little Blue Herons and a solitary American White Pelican. The hunting is intense, because fish dinners will get scarce when the water dries up. Photograph by Bob Gress.

In Cherokee County, down in the extreme south-eastern corner of Kansas, in that environment known as the Ozark Plateau, the Eastern Narrow-mouth Toad patiently awaits the first warm rain of late spring. Up to now, the nights have been too cold, though the cool rains have been a refreshing change from the bitter winds and snow of winter. And then it happens. A toad-strangling gully washer of a storm smashes into the region. The roadside ditches are filled and transformed into miniature wetlands. The male Eastern Narrowmouths eagerly sally forth into the shallows to chorus and lure the females to a tryst. The males sound like a herd of bleating sheep, but to the females they are Pavarotti and Lanza at their finest. Young Narrowmouths are born that same moist and moonless night, another tiny gift from the wetlands of our state. Photograph by Suzanne L. Collins.

The Great Plains Narrowmouth Toad has been much more successful in adapting to the varied Kansas environment than its close cousin, the Eastern Narrow-mouth. This small amphibian lives everywhere in the state and emerges each spring on rainy nights to fill roadside ditches and backyard rainpools. Like its eastern relative, a Great Plains Narrowmouth sounds like a flock of bleating sheep when it calls for its mate. Not exactly a symphony, but apparently an effective enticement to the females, because there is never a shortage of new frogs when the next spring season rolls around. Photograph by Suzanne L. Collins.

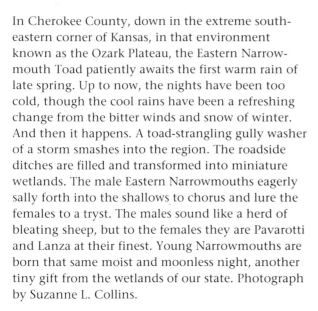

Any recently flooded backwater traps its share of unsuspecting fishes, and the Southern Redbelly Dace is no exception. This school of them hangs out beneath the submerged roots of a tree in a stillwater habitat in Wabaunsee County. When the hot summer arrives, these fish will perish as the water evaporates and their pools shrink to dry hardpan. Raccoons delight in dis-covering such diminishing fish-filled pools. Photograph by Garold Sneegas.

True wetlands, by their temporary nature, have few fishes. But seasonal flooding of oxbow wetlands and woodland floodpools brings an influx of fishes, including this spectacular male Longear Sunfish from a Verdigris River backwater in Chase County. Showy and elegant in his breeding colors, this male Longear could easily grace the aquarium of any fish hobbyist. Indeed, he would hold his own in beauty against most of his tropical relatives. Photograph by Garold Sneegas.

When they fly, Double-crested Cormorants resemble geese. Like geese, they fly in V's or long lines, but Cormorants have faster wingbeats and different silhouettes. Flocks of these birds often settle into flooded timber and wetlands associated with the upper reaches of lakes and ponds. There they catch fish by diving and grabbing them with their slightly hooked beaks. Because their feathers are not entirely waterproof, they are often observed on snags and emergent branches, spreading their soaked wings to dry in the sun. Like the trio shown here, they are quick to take to the water when approached. Photograph by Bob Gress.

Floating Water Primrose blooms from June to September. It grows in shallow water and on muddy banks in bright sunlight. The plants are easy to find because they grow in dense mats, often covered with bright yellow flowers. Mosquitofishes and various minnows like to hide in the tangle of these plants. Northern Cricket Frogs and Plains Leopard Frogs will dive into the foliage at the first sign of an intruder. This probably explains why so many herons and egrets are seen standing motionless among the yellow flowers in ponds and roadside ditches. Photograph by Bob Gress.

In the past, hunters were the main users of Kansas wetlands. During the market hunting of the early 1900s, huge shotguns mounted on wooden boats could slaughter hundreds of ducks. For hunters, a nice flock like the one shown here meant easy money in hard times, but it created hard times for the ducks. Thousands of birds from Cheyenne Bottoms were killed and shipped back to eastern cities, where a dozen Canvasbacks could bring as much as eight dollars. Those days and practices are over. Today, large concentrations of birdlife are still seen at a big marsh like Cheyenne Bottoms, where waterfowl and assorted shorebirds sometimes number in excess of 600,000. Hunting waterfowl is strictly controlled now, and birdwatching has become a favored recreational alternative. Photograph by Mike Blair, Kansas Department of Wildlife and Parks.

A pair of Blue-winged Teal feed in a shallow wetlands by dipping below the surface for a variety of veggies spiced with aquatic insects. Waterfowl that forage in this manner are called dabbling ducks, and include Mallards, Pintails, and Shovelers. When alarmed, dabbling ducks spring straight up from the water in a strong vertical takeoff. Diving ducks, like Redheads, Scaups, and Canvasbacks, use a running start on the water's surface to acquire enough speed for flight. If either kind stuffs itself with too much food, the vertical takeoffs are sometimes weak and the low running starts last a lot longer. Photograph by Bob Gress.

The American Lotus, with its large creamy yellow blossom, is a beautiful member of the water lily family. Its large circular leaves may measure as much as two feet in diameter, providing an ideal perch for frogs, turtles, and aquatic snakes. The plants, which bloom from July to September, sometimes cover many acres of water surface. Largemouth Bass like to wait quietly under these leaves, but anglers are too often discouraged when their lines are constantly snagged on these plants. The long-stemmed brown seed receptacles are commonly seen in dried flower arrangements. The nuts produced in these pods, as well as meaty tubers, were once harvested for food by Native Americans. Photograph by Bob Gress.

Puffed up and popeyed, this pugnacious Plains Spadefoot stands its ground in the temporary waters of a wet meadow. These amphibians are unique among Kansas frogs and toads in having elliptical pupils that close to a slit when exposed to strong light. At night, the pupils open wide and round, and the Plains Spadefoot gains excellent sight and aim, pouncing on any small insects that crawl or fly within reach. Photograph by Suzanne L. Collins.

Although considered a Cajun delicacy, in Kansas the Crayfish is used primarily as bait. Often referred to as "crawdads" or "crawfishes," they are best known for their front legs, modified into large pinchers. Normally, these claws are used as offensive tools for crushing food. When these crustaceans are cornered in a bait container, however, most anglers know the claws also make dandy defensive weapons against tender fingers. When moving along the bottom of a wetland pool, the Crayfish normally walks forward with its five pairs of legs. When alarmed, however, it uses a quick downward jerk of its strong tail and disappears backwards in a swirling cloud of mud. Crayfishes spend a lot of time alarmed and hiding in the murk, because they are a potential dinner for all wetland predators. Photograph by Bob Gress.

The beautiful Black-winged Damselfly is an insect of shady, riparian woodlands. In early summer, the nymph of this delicate creature matures and crawls out of the water where it clings to a plant stem. After drying, a split develops in the back of its thorax and the adult emerges. A few hours later, after the wings are fully dry, the adult flutters off into the woods. There, males defend territories from other males by spreading their wings and raising their abdomens. When females approach, the male spreads its hind wings while holding the front wings folded over its back. For some reason, this really impresses the females. Maybe it's the degree of difficulty. Eventually they mate. She returns to the water to deposit her eggs on plant stems just under the water's surface, and the wetlands cycle begins again. Photograph by Gerald J. Wiens.

A falling water table in the Ogallala Aquifer of western Kansas, caused by out-dated water laws and intensive irrigation, has combined with eastern Colorado reservoirs to destroy most of the Arkansas River in our state. Although the river sometimes flows after exceptionally heavy rains, it more often consists of temporary, drying pools in and along the old river bed, as shown in this autumn scene in Ford County. These pools provide a new wetland habitat for many amphibians, which gladly make use of any standing water in a region known for dry, hot winds that burn the dew from shortgrass so fast that the stems can only dream of tallgrass stature. Photograph by Steve Mulligan.

The Beaver is the largest rodent found in the United States. Easily recognized by its large, flat, scaly tail, an adult Beaver may weigh in excess of sixty pounds and live to be fifteen years old. Beavers do not eat wood, as many people believe, but drop trees to get at the cambium, or growing layer, found just beneath the bark. Not all Beavers build lodges and dams. In Kansas, where the soil is soft, these mammals often tunnel into the bank and live in a chamber with a roof supported by tree roots. Dams are built only on small streams and drainage ditches, where they create temporary wetlands until the Beaver runs out of trees and moves on to a new site. Photograph by Bob Gress.

In spite of decades of poisoning, trapping, and shooting, Coyotes have survived and adapted well to most habitat types in Kansas. Coyotes make regular hunting forays through wetlands, due to the concentration of animal life there. Electric fences are sometimes used to keep them out of the critical nesting habitat of endangered species such as Least Terns and Snowy Plovers. Coyotes are most active early in the morning or late evening, but at night their eerie, yipping chorus proclaims to all ears that they are in tune with the entire Kansas environment. Photograph by Bob Gress.

Minks like water. They have partially webbed toes and can swim like River Otters and live on land like Weasels. They are related to both of these animals, as well as to Skunks and Badgers. Just like their cousins, Minks possess a very effective form of chemical warfare. Although their spray contains just a hint of mint odor, it still is an effective repellent. These small elongate mammals are found in most wetland marshes, where they prey on frogs, crayfishes, fishes, birds, and an occasional Muskrat. Photograph by Bob Gress.

This creature is the most common of all wetland mammals. Muskrats are found in every marsh, oxbow, slough, and pond that manages to maintain some water and a few Cattails. If the water dries up, the Muskrats abandon the wetland and trudge across the land in search of new lodgings, a dangerous trip because many predators like to eat these little fellows. But when rains again fill the wetlands, most Muskrats return for a visit, ready to dig some tunnels among the Cattail roots and dine on crisp greens as well as snails, crayfishes, frogs, and the occasional bird egg. Photograph by Bob Gress.

As summer wears on and the playas, shallowponds, and ditches turn into smaller and smaller puddles of water, the aquatic creatures concentrated in the remaining soup attract a variety of birds and mammals. One of these visitors, the Opossum, is an amazing animal. Its nighttime visits are evident in the tracks left behind in the mud. Unlike the tracks of other animals, tracks made by the hind feet of an Opossum are distinctive because of their backward-pointing thumb. In addition to being the only mammal in our country (other than humans) that possesses a thumb, the Opossum has other unique traits, including a prehensile tail used for grasping, a pouch used to carry its young, and fifty sharp teeth to protect those babies—more dental equipment than any other mammal in North America. Photograph by Bob Gress.

The Raccoon is a highly adaptive, intelligent animal, equally at home searching for food in a Cattail marsh or in an urban trash can. With its sensitive front feet, this nocturnal creature is entertaining to watch as it reaches into every hole along muddy wetland banks, seeking out insects, crayfishes, frogs, tadpoles, snakes, fishes, mice, birds, and bird eggs. Raccoons are omnivorous mammals that will also eat a variety of fruits and seeds. Their ringed tail and black mask make them both easy to identify and appealing. But don't try to touch them—big Raccoons also have big teeth. Photograph by Bob Gress.

Cheyenne Bottoms is the one of the largest inland wetlands in the United States. About six miles northeast of Great Bend, it encompasses about sixty square miles and is the only site in midwestern North America that has been designated a Wetland of International Importance. The Bottoms is considered the most important shorebird migration area in the Western Hemisphere. Estimates indicate that around forty-five percent of the shorebird population east of the 105th meridian stops here during spring migration to refuel on the tiny bloodworms found in the muddy shallows of the big marsh. Until you've visited Cheyenne Bottoms, you cannot know the natural environment of Kansas completely. Photograph by Mike Blair, Kansas Department of Wildlfe and Parks.

Like an angler with a secret fishing spot, the Belted Kingfisher prefers to fish alone. Its territory is usually a small backwater, and the bird defends it fiercely against others of its kind. Upon discovering a good fishing hole, like many anglers, it frequents the site day after day and through all types of weather. Once a Belted Kingfisher spies a possible meal, it flies over the location, hovers, then plunges straight into the water, usually disappearing completely for a moment before returning to the surface with a wiggling catch. The luckless fish is not speared but instead grasped in the open beak of this bird. Belted Kingfishers nest in burrows excavated in banks around waterways. The name "belted" refers to a band or belt of color across the breast. Males have a gray belt; females have that and a second brownish-colored belt. Photograph by Bob Gress.

The American Avocet is one of the largest and most distinctive of wetland shorebirds. The long, slender upturned bill, long legs, long neck, and striking black and white pattern on its back and sides make it easy to identify. The bill is used in an unusual manner. These birds, either singly or in flocks, walk slowly through shallow water sweeping the bill from side to side. The upturned bill stirs up aquatic insects, which are snapped up with the partly opened beak. This American Avocet was photographed near its nest on the sun-baked salt flats of Quivira National Wildlife Refuge. Within fifty feet were the nests of a Black-necked Stilt, a Killdeer, a Snowy Plover, and two pairs of Least Terns, a living tribute to the value of this unique habitat. Photograph by Bob Gress.

The American Bittern is a shy heron that hunts by stalking fish, frogs, and crayfish in dense stands of Cattails and rushes of wetlands. Its vertically streaked plumage makes it very difficult to see when it stands motionless with its bill pointed skyward. If the Cattails are blowing in the breeze, the crafty bittern will also sway back and forth in time with the movement. The American Bittern is sometimes called a "thunder pumper" because of its low-pitched, three-syllable "pump-er-lunk" song, which can carry for more than a half mile on a warm spring day. Photograph by Bob Gress.

Many Kansans refer to the American Coot as a "mudhen," probably because it frequents shallow muddy waters of wetlands and is shaped like a small chicken. It is a common bird and is sometimes seen swimming in large flocks. From a distance it appears black, but up close its plumage is slate gray. With its short white bill it eats aquatic plants as well as insects, tadpoles, small fishes, and snails. When swimming, it chugs along with its head pumping back and forth. Takeoff is an exciting moment to watch; it begins with the bird running and splashing along the surface of the water for some distance with its wings beating vigorously. It ends with the birdwatchers holding their breath as the little fellow finally becomes airborne. Photograph by Bob Gress.

The green vegetation along the borders of oxbows and railroad ditches is an excellent place to look for the graceful, agile Rough Green Snake. Seeing them, however, is another matter, because they blend so well with the background. These gentle, harmless serpents love humid habitats, where they bask in the sun and dine on passing insects. Photograph by Suzanne L. Collins.

Our national bird, the Bald Eagle, is back. In the last decade, hundreds of these raptors have begun to migrate to Kansas in winter, spending much time around the ice-free shallows of our waterways. In pioneer days, there were sketchy references to Bald Eagles nesting in our state. Since those days, dozens of reservoirs have been constructed, and most of their upper reaches feature shallow wetlands with abundant tall, dead trees, ideal for nesting eagles. Recently, several pairs of eagles have built winter nests and stayed to raise their young, particularly in the wetlands arm of Clinton Lake. With more habitat now available in Kansas, and assuming limited disturbance, nesting Bald Eagles may be a part of our future. The bird in this photograph has lost a toe, perhaps to a trap, but is otherwise doing quite well. Photograph by Bob Gress.

A summer thunderstorm at noon darkens the Neosho Wildlife Area. Sensing the weather change, Turkey Vultures gathered on the dead trees in the shallow wetland arm of the marsh to ride out the turbulence. After the rain ended, they sat in the warming sun, fresh and clean, until their feathers were dry, and then cruised off to the nearby highway to look for a roadkill lunch. Photograph by Suzanne L. Collins.

Evening sky darkens as an advancing thunderstorm moves toward an Egret nesting colony in central Kansas. The restless birds swarm into the air, almost as if they sense a change in pressure. With a blast of wind and driving rain the front moves in, and the long clenched toes of 15,000 Egrets hang onto the Cattails. Moments later, the sky is empty and calm. Even without the exciting conditions of a storm, the evening flights of birds during summer months are spectacular to watch. Photograph by Bob Gress.

When the other herons head back to the wetlands heronry to roost at sunset, the Black-crowned Night Heron is just leaving to feed. It's a noisy bird, and anyone who's ever heard its call will understand why this creature used to be called a "squawk." Its eyes are bright red and quite large, the latter probably an adaptation to its nocturnal habits, the former maybe because it stays out too late partying on the pond. Whatever the reasons, knowledgeable folks think these birds may have adopted nighttime feeding as a way to escape harassment from the more numerous herons that are active by day. Photograph by Bob Gress.

Unlike some wetlands shorebirds, the Black-necked Stilt is a conspicuous and easily observed resident of shallow marshes and flooded fields. With its long neck and long skinny legs, the stilt resembles an American Avocet. Unlike the Avocet, whose bill is upturned and hooked at the tip, the Stilt's bill is arrow straight and needle sharp. One of the Stilt's striking features is its ten-inch-long pink or reddish legs. It walks gracefully with long strides, and is also a fast runner. Around its nesting area, it is very noisy, often screeching and buzzing like a small fighter pilot at any possible nest invader. Photograph by Bob Gress.

The Slider is probably the only aquatic turtle in Kansas that benefits from the creation of a huge reservoir. Once the big dam is in place and the lake fills, the shallow end becomes a stillwater lagoon surrounded by a shoreline of luxuriant plant life. Against this green backdrop the naked trunks and limbs of tall trees stand as mute testimony that too much water can kill. Eventually, the dead trees begin to fall, creating log jams and stumps that make sunning spots galore for the Slider and other wetland wildlife. Photograph by Suzanne L. Collins.

An arid land pioneer, the Yellow Mud Turtle is one of the few aquatic turtles that has adapted well to the playas and often-dry wetlands of the western half of Kansas. When the temporary shallows of the plains go dry, the Yellow Mud Turtle digs down in the mud deep enough to cover its shell and stays hidden from the merciless heat of the sun until the rains return. Then it emerges and once again haunts the all too transient western waters, ready to deal with the cycle of wet-dry-wet many times during its life. Photograph by Suzanne L. Collins.

This water-filled ditch along a railroad right-of-way in Cherokee County is a warm, humid environment, its slopes lined with discarded wooden ties that sizzle in the heat of a noonday sun. A female Broadhead Skink digs a cavity beneath a railroad tie, lays her eggs, and guards them, secure from most predators. When they hatch, the bright yellow-and-black striped baby lizards will scamper under and about the detritus that lines this wetland. On reaching adulthood, they will wander away and climb into large trees, but the females will always return to the slope of the ditch to lay their eggs; it's a good place to raise a family. Photograph by Suzanne L. Collins.

The Green Toad is the smallest of Kansas toads, a mere pip-squeak when lined up with the more ponderous Great Plains, American, and Woodhouse's varieties. In keeping with its size, this toad's call is not much more than a weak buzz. This matters little, because the Green Toad choruses and thrives only on the High Plains in the western fifth of the state, where an audience can be a bit sparse. Photograph by Suzanne L. Collins.

Most widespread of Kansas toads, the Woodhouse's Toad spends most of its spring in wet meadows, backyard rainpools, and roadside ditches, where it sings and swims at night in search of a willing mate. After breeding is completed, these amphibians become much more terrestrial and move near more permanent water to enjoy the warm humid nights of summer and burrow in the moist mud or sand during the hot day. Photograph by Suzanne L. Collins.

Gray is not the only suit of this amphibian. It can quickly turn bright green given the proper stimulus of a matching background. During late spring, Gray Treefrogs breed in forested floodpools and backwaters. In summer, they often climb high into trees and bask directly in the sun, one of the few frogs that can withstand such exposure. These frogs do not have many enemies, because they blend so well with their surroundings and their skin secretes a distasteful toxin that irritates a predator's mucous membranes. If you catch and hold one of these delightful little amphibians, be sure to wash your hands afterwards. Photograph by Suzanne L. Collins.

Like most chorus frogs, this green-spotted amphibian spends much of the year hidden beneath leaves and other debris. Come spring on the prairies, and these little amphibians make straight for the wetland pools and ditches that fill with rain. There they sing and breed, expending enormous amounts of energy in vigorous pursuit of a mate. After the eggs are laid and fertilized in the water, the Spotted Chorus Frog disappears once again, hidden from most danger, husbanding its re-sources while the seasons cycle, ready to go at the next spring fling with renewed stamina. Photograph by Suzanne L. Collins.

Duckweed is a tiny plant commonly found floating on quiet waters throughout the state. As its name suggests, it is sometimes consumed in large quantities by ducks. These plants and their relatives are the smallest flowering plants in the world. Under good conditions, Duckweed may completely cover a woodland pool or small pond during the course of a summer. The plants rarely flower, reproducing instead by buds that break off and grow new plants. Many wetland creatures value Duckweed, because they can hide beneath it and snare unsuspecting prey. Photograph by Bob Gress.

The Franklin's Gull is named after Sir John Franklin, an English explorer of the Arctic. Although many people refer to all gulls as "sea gulls," the Franklin's Gull is a bird of the Great Plains and prairies, not the high seas. During the spring and fall months, large, loosely knit flocks of these gulls migrate across Kansas. They feed mostly on insects and are often spotted following along behind the plows or disks of farmers, plucking up unearthed cutworms and grubs. Flocks of these birds often gather to rest on sand bars and wetland mudflats. This resting pair displays their striking black heads and red beaks. Photograph by Bob Gress.

The Great Blue Heron, often misidentified as a crane by the novice birdwatcher, is the most commonly seen wetland bird in Kansas. It is also the largest, and its nesting colonies are usually well known to local residents. Many of these colonies are used continually for years and may number over a hundred nests. In eastern Kansas, nesting colonies, or rookeries, are usually located in the tallest Sycamore trees growing from the bottoms of local streams and rivers. In western Kansas, the nests are usually placed in Cottonwood trees. A wary bird, the Great Blue Heron is found throughout the state, often fishing alone along the edges of marshes, ponds, lakes, and streams. Photograph by Bob Gress.

All egrets are herons, but not all herons are egrets. An egret is simply a white-colored heron. In Kansas, there are three kinds of egrets, and the immature Little Blue Heron is also white. The Great Egret is the largest of the egrets found in our state, and the only one with black legs and feet and a yellow bill. With its longer legs, this big bird is able to fish in wetland waters too deep for other kinds of herons. Great Egrets are rather aggressive, and if another bird gets too close, a brief chase helps reestablish the proper allocation of fishing territory. Photograph by Bob Gress.

The Green-backed Heron is a retiring bird of small wooded streams, drainage ditches, and wetland marshes. Unlike many herons, the Green-backed is usually solitary both in feeding and nesting. Its dark coloring blends well when feeding from a snag under the shade of a tree. Though these birds often catch their prey in conventional heron manner, they also can be quite acrobatic. For example, in deeper water, this small heron will wait patiently from an overhanging branch watching the water closely. When a small fish swims by, the Green-backed Heron will launch itself like a spear while holding on tightly with its feet. Stretched upside down with its head and neck under the water, the bird is momentarily in an embarrassing and most unbirdlike stance. But dignity is restored when it pulls itself back up, and there is usually a small fish clutched in its bill. Photograph by Bob Gress.

The Greater Yellowlegs gets its name for the obvious reason shown here. It is a very wary bird, often the first bird to flush when an intruder walks the shoreline, and its ringing cry startles other shorebirds into the air. It is usually found on wetland mudflats, but unlike other long-billed shorebirds, it does not use its beak to probe the mud. Instead, the Greater Yellowlegs walks along and uses its beak like tweezers to daintily pick insects and other small animals from the water's surface. It nests in the far north but is regularly seen in Kansas wetlands during migration. Photograph by Bob Gress.

Ahhhh! Nothing like a long warm soak in the shallows before an evening of insect hunting. Green Frogs aren't very green and don't normally appear so, unless they are lounging in Duckweed, like the one shown here. These amphibians are found only in Cherokee County, down in extreme southeastern Kansas. Each spring season they get together and put on a show at the local oxbow or slough. Their chorus is startling to those who haven't heard it, sounding just like a bunch of twanging banjos, a sort of damp down-home deliverance from the winter doldrums. Photograph by Suzanne L. Collins.

An approaching spring storm will help recharge the water supply of Big Salt Marsh in Quivira National Wildlife Refuge. All Kansas waterways experience seasonal fluctuations in water levels. During the summer season, true wetlands go completely dry, and droughts may keep them that way for several years. When water is once again abundant, wetland plants, whose seeds have lain dormant in the hard dry soils, reappear in great numbers. Photograph by Bob Gress.

The Least Bittern is not only the smallest member of the heron family but also one of the shiest. It is difficult to find this bird unless an observer is dedicated enough to wade through Cattail marsh after Cattail marsh until one is flushed from its hiding place. The startled bird appears to fly awkwardly with its neck outstretched and its legs dangling. Sometimes the Least Bittern will hide by freezing, standing perfectly motionless with its bill pointed skyward. These young birds were only one day old and already showed the beginnings of this behavior, not the least concerned about their appearance. After all, even a Least Bittern can have a bad hair day. Photograph by Bob Gress.

An egg from the endangered interior race of the Least Tern is more precious than gold. There is certainly more gold bullion produced every year than there are Least Tern eggs. These birds have been placed in a precarious position because of habitat loss, the same factor threatening other wetland species. This is the smallest of the terns found in Kansas. The best place to look for it is at Quivira National Wildlife Refuge. Least Terns nest there along the salt flats during the summer months, but do not disturb them. As an endangered species, they are protected by law from any type of disturbance, direct or indirect. Photograph by Bob Gress.

Adult Little Blue Herons like the one shown here are strikingly different in coloring from the immature birds. Unlike any other dark-colored herons, the young Little Blues are snow white in color. After a year, the white immatures begin to molt into adult plumage a few feathers at a time. Birds with some white and some blue feathers are sometimes called "piebald" or "pied herons." During winter, Little Blue Herons migrate as far as South America in search of warmer climes. Photograph by Bob Gress.

Long-billed Dowitchers are chunky, snipe-like sandpipers with bills nearly three inches long. They fly in flocks and are fun to watch as they feed in shallow water and soft wetland mudflats. Their feeding behavior has been likened to the action of a sewing machine. As they walk along the shoreline, their bodies are like the base on which the machine rests, relatively motionless, while their heads and vertical beaks pump up and down like a sewing needle, rapidly probing the mud for food. Resting birds commonly turn their heads and bury the long beak in the feathers down the middle of the back. Photograph by Bob Gress.

The Mallard is the most recognized and the most abundant of all ducks. There may be as many as nine million of these birds in North America alone. A large domestic race is frequently raised on farms and is often seen around urban lakes and rivers. The wild Mallard is a favorite target for waterfowl hunters across the wetlands of our nation. Males are easily recognized by their metallic green head, while the females are a basic brown. Female Mallards pluck soft down from their breast to line the nest and lay about a dozen eggs. After an incubation period of four weeks, the precocious young follow Mom to the nearest source of water for their first dip. Photograph by Bob Gress.

The Marbled Godwit is a large shorebird nearly the size of a duck, and with its five-inch upturned bill, it stands out in the shoreline crowd. The bill is used to probe deeply in mud for insect larvae and worms. Its large body size made this bird a popular target for market hunters in the 1800s, and Godwits, along with Long-billed Curlews, were slaughtered in huge numbers. Today these birds are protected and doing just fine. They visit Kansas wetlands during their seasonal migration as they cruise north to breeding grounds on the grassy northern prairies. Keep an eye out for this bird at Quivira National Wildlife Refuge and Cheyenne Bottoms. Photograph by Bob Gress.

This bird used to be called a "marsh hawk," due to its preference for hunting over marshes, sloughs, wet meadows, and wetland prairies. The male, shown here, is pale gray, and females are predominantly brown. Both sexes are slim, long-tailed, and long-legged, with an obvious white rump patch. Their face is almost owl-like in appearance. Unlike most hawks, the Northern Harrier nests on the ground, often near low shrubs or tall grasses and usually close to wetlands. When hunting, it flies low over a marsh with a few wing beats, followed by a swift, buoyant glide from which it drops silent and unsuspecting on mice, frogs, crayfishes, snakes, and many kinds of insects. Photograph by Bob Gress.

The Marsh Wren is rarely found outside its wetland habitat of Cattails, rushes, reeds, and tall marsh grasses. It is very secretive and difficult to observe. Always in motion, moving mouselike through the Cattails, it occasionally peeks out at an observer. It rarely nests in Kansas, but if you discover a globelike nest with an entrance on the side about three feet high in the Cattails, count yourself lucky. For birdwatchers, the Marsh Wren is always an excellent find, and the nest is a big bonus. Photograph by Bob Gress.

A male Ruddy Duck is, at all times, dapper. But in breeding colors, he is stunning, with a bright blue bill, white cheek, and bright ruddy plumage. From a distance, the male Ruddy is easily recognized in silhouette with his erect, stiff tail. When courting, the male shows off by puffing out his chest, bowing, and bobbing his head rapidly. The female is much more subtle in coloring and decorum. Both are small, weighing a maximum of about one pound. When nesting, the female lays huge eggs, nearly the size of those laid by a fifteen-pound wild Turkey. The nest may contain up to eight eggs, a staggering output from such a small duck. Weary from the effort, a female sometimes deposits her eggs in the nests of other waterfowl and lets them take over the responsibilities of motherhood. Photograph by Bob Gress.

Crawfish Frogs have this thing about crayfishes. They like to move in with a crayfish unannounced and remodel the entrance to the burrow by adding a flat sunporch. Next they dig out a side chamber and widen the opening. Pretty soon there's simply not enough room for both, so the crayfish has to leave. Rumor has it that some crayfishes provide the ultimate in hospitality before they have a chance to depart. That is, they become dinner for the Crawfish Frog, hungry from all that work. The frog clearly has the better part of the deal and, like this female, lives secure in a crayfish burrow in the wet lowland meadows of eastern Kansas. Photograph by Suzanne L. Collins.

Trying to find a Western Chorus Frog on a wet spring night can be frustrating in the extreme. These little amphibians like to sing beneath a dead leaf or under brown matted grass stems, usually near or in a wetlands. But grass stems and dead leaves are rather common, on the order of several zillion per marsh or ditch. As if this weren't enough of a hardship in the hunt, the Western Chorus Frog also can effectively misdirect its voice, causing would-be predators, including frog catchers, to spend much wasted time bent over peering under leaves in a cold rain. Little wonder that this pastime has not yet caught on. Photograph by Suzanne L. Collins.

A Black Willow Tree along one of the nature trails at Chisholm Creek Park in Wichita is shade for frogs and other small creatures. This park is a good area to birdwatch, count butterflies, photograph aquatic insects, or just take the sun. Recreational activities are on the upswing at all wilderness areas, but the peace, tranquillity, and escape from everyday stress that they can afford is threatened by overuse—too many people and too few acres of natural environment, particularly quiet, sleepy wetlands. Photograph by Bob Gress.

Beavers are the only creatures other than people that can actually create wetlands. When shallow streams, such as this one at McPherson State Fishing Lake, are colonized by these semi-aquatic mammals, they immediately cut down trees, build dams, and create pools to provide themselves with security and watery routes to favorite feeding areas. In the process, the pools act as catch basins for water and sediment. The mix of water and sediment is fertile, and soon Cattails, Willows, and other aquatic plants make an appearance around the water line. All this vegetation around water makes for a varied habitat, and other wildlife shows up to take advantage of it. Soon the entire place is filled with plants and animals trying to make a living. And all of this evolved because a Beaver had this notion. Photograph by Bob Gress.

The chortling calls of migrating Sandhill Cranes are almost always heard before the birds are seen. They call constantly to keep the flock together. Unlike herons, cranes fly with their necks outstretched and their long legs trailing. Sandhill Cranes eat a wide variety of foods, ranging from mice, snakes, frogs, and insects to corn and milo. They are very cautious and usually will not allow observers to approach closer than several hundred yards. At night, migrating flocks of these birds settle into marshes, where they stand in shallow water. The small flock of Sandhill Cranes shown here was photographed just before sunrise, only moments before the birds flew to adjacent grain fields for an early morning breakfast. Photograph by Bob Gress.

The Sora is a member of the rail family and a denizen of wetland marshes across the state. Most of the time it is very secretive and difficult to see as it moves silently through thick vegetation in shallow water. Sometimes, however, it seems to undergo a personality change and decides to walk around in full view of everyone, calling loudly. Its feet are big, reminiscent of oversized clown feet. The toes make it easy for this small bird to walk or run lightly across floating vegetation, but they haven't yet evolved to permit it to walk on water. The Sora is a classy traveler, wintering in the West Indies and Bermuda. Not for this bird the bitter cold of a Kansas wetland in winter. Photograph by Bob Gress.

A sparrow-sized Snowy Plover is nearly invisible when resting at its nesting area on white salt flats. It takes great pains to ensure that its eggs are also difficult to see. To make a place for the eggs, the male digs a shallow scrape and then the female lines it with small stones, selected to match the color of her eggs. She usually lays three eggs in mid June to early July, and they hatch after an incubation period of around twenty-four days. The chick shown here hatched only a few hours before the photograph was taken. A short while later, three precocious young wobbled away on toothpick-sized legs, following their calling parent and eager to see the wetlands world around them. Photograph by Bob Gress.

Denizen of roadsides ditches and flooded woodlands on rainy spring nights, the Small-mouth Salamander inhabits the water-rich eastern third of Kansas. Prevented from invading the western part of Kansas by the comparatively dry and open Flint Hills, this nondescript little amphibian has fully exploited the forested wetlands of the Osage Cuestas. Here it flourishes, because of the abundant temporary water in which to lay its eggs and watch its larvae thrive. But crossing the roads to get to these low, wet places is dangerous, and many Smallmouths die in the attempt. Maybe we need new designs for our roads that favor wildlife as well as vehicles. Maybe we need special tunnels beneath the roads. Many other creatures would benefit along with the salamanders. Think about it the next time you see a road-killed baby Raccoon or young Red Fox. Photograph by Suzanne L. Collins.

Hardiest of pioneers among the Kansas salamander fauna, the versatile Tiger Salamander is the only species that has settled nearly the entire state. Unlike most Kansas salamanders, these amphibians can live in or near a wide variety of aquatic habitats—farm ponds, roadside ditches, flooded woodlands, oxbows, and marshes. In addition, they have learned to use Prairie Dog burrows and caves to escape the hot summer sun and avoid fatal desiccation. They are also opportunists, patiently waiting for rainfall in a state where the impatient don't make it. We suspect that, in ancient times, many a Kansas Tiger Salamander, not much different from today's model, watched in amusement as lesser types challenged the arid environment and lost. The Tiger just sat there and waited. And watched. And won. Photograph by Suzanne L. Collins.

A distasteful skin secretion makes the Eastern Newt an exciting dining experience for greedy predators that display bad table manners and gobble what they eat. Fortunately for this salamander, most of its enemies have learned their lesson and give it a wide berth. Adult Eastern Newts spend much of the time floating in small woodland pools and backwaters, dining on insects, and courting each other. A newborn Newt is aquatic, like its parents, but soon metamorphoses into a land-dwelling creature called an "eft." It spends its formative years on land in the moist world beneath big rocks and rotten fallen logs. Eventually, the eft returns to the water, transforms to adulthood, and is ready to begin the cycle anew. Photograph by Suzanne L. Collins.

Duck hunters sometimes call the White-fronted Goose a "specklebelly" because of the markings shown here. It actually gets the name "white-fronted" from the white seen on the front of its face just above the bill. The bird also has a white rear end, but this was apparently overlooked when common names were handed out. In Kansas, this bird is present only during spring and fall migrations. It nests in northern Alaska and Canada. White-fronted Geese feed on aquatic vegetation and insects as well as grain left in fields after a harvest. Photograph by Bob Gress.

The male Wood Duck, the most stunningly beautiful duck in North America, lives in most forested wetlands in the eastern half of Kansas. Wood Ducks nest in the cavities of hollow trees, sometimes as high as fifty feet above the ground. After bursting from their eggs, the rambunctious young ducklings are restless, and quickly respond to Mom's persistent calling by climbing to the cavity entrance. With only a slight pause and a little teetering, each makes a giant leap, tumbling head over heels. Then the young ducks bounce up and race after their very frantic mother. Very few are injured from the harrowing jump, but Mom probably still views them as irresponsible youngsters. Photograph by Bob Gress.

When people first encounter the Yellow-headed Blackbird, they're often convinced that they've just seen an exotic escapee from the local zoo. But these beautiful birds are common in Kansas. In the spring, large flocks descend on fields in search of insects and seeds. The males migrate first, so some flocks, like this one, consist entirely of males. When confronted by a rival, the male Yellowhead fluffs up his head and neck, fans his tail, and emits a screech that sounds something like the distant squeal of a hog. Apparently, this is intimidating to other males; the impression it makes on a female Yellowhead is uncertain. Photograph by Bob Gress.

The Yellow-crowned Night Heron is much less common in Kansas than its cousin, the Black-crowned. Its usual haunts are the coastal areas of the southeastern United States, where it dines on delicacies such as crab. In our state, it substitutes crayfishes for crabs. Although seen occasionally in the wetland marshes of the state, it's found most regularly feeding along the backwaters near some of our larger cities. In Wichita, a half dozen nests are reported every year in the tall trees of people's backyards. There, the birds gaze down on barbecues that probably do not feature Cajun cuisine such as crayfishes, and squawk their displeasure. Photograph by Bob Gress.

Canvasbacks are diving ducks, often found feeding on submerged vegetation in the shallow marshy areas of wetlands, particularly near Cattails and rushes. They are well known for their tendency to choose a neighbor's nest as a "dump nest," a sort of communal nest where other female Canvasbacks can slip in unnoticed and lay a few eggs. Of course, the nest's owners are stuck with raising ducklings for the whole neighborhood, unknowingly providing an avian duckcare center for free. Photograph by Bob Gress.

In summer, the Common Goldeneye spends its time up north, nesting in the tree cavities of coniferous forests that border water. During fall and winter, however, it frequents the larger wetlands of Kansas. Even when that water freezes, some of these birds still spurn the flight south, remaining behind on small patches of open water in nearby ice-choked rivers. There they entertain delighted birdwatchers with an elaborate social display. Photograph by Bob Gress.

Like most snakes, the Plainbelly Water Snake avoids people. This is good, because people really shouldn't fool around with these serpents. It's not that they are dangerous; they're just antisocial. When caught, they make their displeasure known, instantly biting the closest hand or arm and simultaneously evacuating their bowels all over the unwary captor. Those who have captured these harmless creatures for sport would swear that the snakes bit them with relish. The authors don't grab them anymore, but we love to watch young herpetologists pick them up barehanded for the first time. Photograph by Suzanne L. Collins.

Denizen of still and shallow backwaters in the southeastern part of the state, this smallest of Kansas turtles offers an unpleasant surprise. When handled, it gets excited; when excited, it emits a disagreeable odor from small glands beneath its upper shell at the rear edge. This causes most folks to put the turtle back in the water and observe it from a more pleasant distance. Hardy individuals who hold their noses and continue to hold the Common Musk Turtle will soon discover that it's a snappy little fellow, quite willing to nip fingers that stray too close to its head. Photograph by Suzanne L. Collins.

Once a rarity in Kansas, Canada Geese now appear to be firmly established on most waterways statewide, including the wetlands arms of reservoirs, due to restocking efforts by the Kansas Department of Wildlife and Parks. The local populations are still supplemented by large migratory flocks during the fall and winter. In spring, after the migratory birds move back north, the local residents can be found nesting. A female Canada Goose lays four to six eggs and defends them fiercely. Her beak is powerful enough to raise a blood blister (based on personal experience) and her wings can beat like a club on anyone who gets too close to the nest. Even a Raccoon would rather find something easier to eat than goose eggs. The eggs in this nest are just hatching. Within a day, the female will lead her young off to water, abandoning the nest. Photograph by Bob Gress.

Originally at home following the herds of grazing animals on the plains of Africa, the Cattle Egret joined the hordes of immigrants to America's shores and is now a common sight in our country. Like many seeking a new and better home, it came here on its own, probably in a single flight across the Atlantic Ocean. It was first seen in South America in the late 1800s. Next, the bird found its way to Florida in 1941. Finally, the Cattle Egret reached the Kansas plains in 1964 and felt right at home. It found that cattle are just as good at flushing up grasshoppers and spiders for dinner as the water buffalo and gazelle in its native Africa. The Cattle Egret now nests in several areas around the state and is a common, and lovely, sight. Photograph by Bob Gress.

With its heavy body, stubby legs, and big pouch, the American White Pelican has long been popular as a caricature, its likeness appearing on commercial items ranging from tote bags to trash cans. The Pelican's skin pouch is a handy tool that functions much like a dip net. Pelicans fishing will often swim in lines, working together to concentrate a school of fish—their intended lunch—within a closing circle of birds or against the wetlands shoreline. Once entrapped, the fishes are scooped up with a bill that can hold up to four gallons of water. After emptying the water, these big birds gulp down their catch and the skin pouch shrinks back into their lower mandibles. At dusk, as the Pelicans prepare to return to their evening roost, carryout snacks are the rule. Photograph by Bob Gress.

Racers haunt wetlands, looking for food. These serpents glide slowly around lowland pools and ditches and are quick to detect the slightest movement of a salamander, frog, insect, or rodent hiding in the vegetation that sprouts when wetlands spring to life after a good solid rain. Racers are fast, aggressive, and alert, and at first they don't take kindly to being handled by people. After a while, they calm down some and can be held and examined. They always stay a little nervous, though, and are obviously glad to be released, slipping swiftly away in the grass. Photograph by Suzanne L. Collins.

From the standpoint of girth, the Diamondback Water Snake is hefty. It's also harmless, but it sure doesn't appear that way to a startled angler who accidentally meets one of these big reptiles while night fishing on the bank of an eastern Kansas oxbow or backwater slough. Like all water snakes, the Diamondback spends much of a night slowly cruising the shoreline in search of an occasional frog; more importantly, it readily eats any dead fishes it finds and thereby helps to keep the place clean. Anglers should ponder that before succumbing to the primeval kneejerk reaction of their ancestors and killing the snake with any handy weapon. Photograph by Suzanne L. Collins.

Snappers are aggressive, tough turtles, rugged reptiles built to withstand the most demanding times. Unlike most of their aquatic brethren, they like to stomp about and are avid wanderers, frequently on the go from lake to river to pond in search of permanent water. Temporary wetlands provide them an excellent way station, a place to float in the warm water, snack on a duckling or frog, and take the sun. Eventually, the shoreline shrinks and the water disappears, and the Snapping Turtle must haul out on land to face the rigors of another march in its search for a more stable home. Photograph by Suzanne L. Collins.

Located only twenty miles south of Cheyenne Bottoms, Quivira National Wildlife Refuge may provide the best opportunity for viewing birdlife in Kansas. Nearly all of the wetland species found at the Bottoms are also found here, and the Wildlife Drive along the north end of the refuge provides easy access to the salt flats, shallow pools, and cattail marshes of Big Salt Marsh. The salt inhibits plant growth and makes visible large numbers of herons, shorebirds, and waterfowl as they feed in the shallow water. Seen here are Long-billed Dowitchers, Snowy Egrets, and Franklin's Gulls. Photograph by Bob Gress.

Unlike the Plains Leopard Frog, Southern Leopard Frogs do not tolerate dry western Kansas. These colorful frogs live in the southeastern part of the state, where rain is more plentiful and wetlands more numerous. They are particularly fond of the roadside ditches and swamps around the Marais des Cygnes Wildlife Area, where large choruses can be heard on warm spring nights. Photograph by Suzanne L. Collins.

So slender it easily lives up to its name, this skinny ribbon of a serpent glides swiftly through a forested floodpool in search of small frogs. Although a close relative of garter snakes, the Western Ribbon Snake is much more dependent on wetlands for food and refuge from enemies. Young Ribbon Snakes look like little stems or reeds and are so small that most large predators probably overlook them. Photograph by Suzanne L. Collins.

The Common Garter Snake really is common in eastern Kansas, but its range stops at the High Plains. It is a wetlands serpent, at home along roadside ditches, wet meadows, and oxbows, where it hunts for small fishes, salamanders, frogs, and toads. When wetlands are healthy, this reptile does well. It may produce up to eighty young per brood in a good year, which makes for quite an extended family. Photograph by Suzanne L. Collins.

Snappy citizen of swamps, low meadows, and other wetland habitats, the Massasauga nowhere reaches greater abundance than in Cheyenne Bottoms. There it thrives on the slopes of the dikes, hunting frogs and rodents. Although venomous, as far as we know its bite has never proven fatal to anyone in Kansas, though a bite by one of these small snakes demands medical treatment. Massasaugas have provided, and will continue to provide, duck hunters with some of their most exciting moments at the Bottoms. Imagine the scene. A cool early morning. The hunters have been dropped at a blind well out in the waterfowl pool. The boat leaves and is soon out of hearing range. Then one of the hunters discovers a drowsy, chilled Massasauga curled in the blind. It's all there—uninformed people, a confined space, guns, and a twenty-three-inch catalyst called "Rattlesnake!" The chemistry is just right for an unfortunate and harmless encounter to become a legendary tale, to be told and retold around the campfires of future duck hunters. Photograph by Suzanne L. Collins.

Although there is an autumn hunting season on Virginia Rails, few of the birds are taken during the fall, because they take evasive action, refusing to flush, preferring to run through cold inhospitable marshes and sometimes taking directly to the water. When they do decide to fly, it's usually for only a short distance and appears to be quite awkward with slow fluttering wings and dangling legs. This bird has a variety of odd calls ranging from metallic clicks to pig-like grunts, causing hunters to ponder what awaits them in the shoreline vegetation. The Virginia Rail eats insects and small fishes. The best way to observe this bird is to sit motionless on the edge of a marsh, scanning the edges for a slight movement, and hoping your muscles don't cramp. Photograph by Bob Gress.

The strange honking calls of the White-faced Ibis seem to be perfectly matched to birds with such unusual beaks. While feeding, they use these long down-curved bills to diligently probe the wetlands mudpools for juicy worms, insects, crayfishes, frogs, and occasionally fishes. Flying Ibises present an unforgettable view as they float in slow wavering lines with their legs and necks extended. The birds appear black from a distance, but as they come closer they reveal chestnut brown feathers with an iridescent sheen of green and violet. In Kansas, these birds prefer semipermanent wetlands such as Quivira National Wildlife Refuge and Cheyenne Bottoms. Photograph by Bob Gress.

Many small lakes in Kansas, like this one in Atchison County, are very shallow and support a thick concentration of lily pads. Although not true wetlands, these impoundments are on a successional trajectory to become modest versions of them. Silt pours in after every rainfall, and the bottom mud of these ponds gets deeper and higher until the roots of aquatic plants catch hold and thrive. Eventually, when the water is only a few inches deep, it begins to dry up periodically, and a miniature primordial Cheyenne Bottoms appears. At that point, the diversity and number of wildlife living in and around the wetlands habitat reach a level that the former small lake could never support. Photograph by Suzanne L. Collins.

The American Toad is a habitat snob, as toads go, because it prefers to live in wooded upland areas where it can look down on its cousins living in the mud and uncertainty of floodplains. These amphibians prefer the forested pools and roadside ditches of ridges and hills in eastern Kansas. There they spend the summer nights snaring insects and watching the woodland world go about its nocturnal business. By day, this warty creature retreats beneath leaves, logs, and rocks to avoid the sun's heat. Photograph by Suzanne L. Collins.

An evening of hunting insects is the same as Saturday night on the town for the Great Plains Toad, a familiar amphibian across the lowland prairies of much of western Kansas. These small creatures can often be found of an evening, stolidly squatting together beneath the lone street lamp of a small Kansas town, gazing raptly skyward as if counting the stars. Actually, they are probably gazing much closer to home, counting the insects flying around the lamp. Many of those insects fall to earth, where the toads make some remarkable one-bounce catches. Photograph by Suzanne L. Collins.

The Common Moorhen is found almost worldwide, except in Australia and Antarctica. In Kansas, it frequents marshes, mostly in the eastern half of the state. Most of the breeding records are from around Cheyenne Bottoms and Quivira National Wildlife Refuge. This bird behaves much like an American Coot, swimming along the edges of Cattails and dipping its head under water to pull up aquatic vegetation, its preferred food. Sometimes it is seen walking around on land, feeding much like a chicken. The Moorhen shown here blushingly displays its most distinctive characteristic, a yellow beak that changes to bright red on its head. Photograph by Bob Gress.

Most warblers are normally associated with woodlands. The Common Yellowthroat, however, is a bird that prefers marshy wetland areas. It's right at home in the Cattails, where it sings a "witchity, witchity, witchity" song. The Yellowthroat is a shy and cautious bird, disappearing silently into the Cattails at the first sign of an intruder, and then reappearing to vigorously scold— from a safer distance. Like other warblers, it feeds primarily on the insects that are always in abundance at any wetlands. Photograph by Bob Gress.

Wet grassy areas around ponds and drainage ditches are ideal locations for flushing the Common Snipe during spring and fall months. When approached, these birds usually remain motionless until they are right at your feet, and then flush wildly, giving their sharp "snipe" call as they zip away. The long beak of the Common Snipe is used to probe for worms and grubs. The tip of the beak is soft and full of nerve endings, allowing the birds to feel for prey. On its northern nesting grounds, the Snipe is well known for its spectacular courtship flight. In a power dive from great heights, the outer tail feathers vibrate and produce a hollow, whistling sound known as "winnowing," a sound that can be heard for a half mile. Photograph by Bob Gress.

Woodland floodpools in extreme southeastern Kansas are the perfect habitat for this noisy little frog. When Spring Peepers get together in large numbers, they can set up quite a racket. Unfortunately, our state has only a few habitats where such vernal choruses can be heard, but if these are protected, the wonderful song of this small amphibian will remain a part of our natural heritage for future generations—of both frogs and people. Photograph by Suzanne L. Collins.

The Strecker's Chorus Frog is one of the rarest amphibians in Kansas, mostly because its habitat requirements are so strict. It lives only in south-central Kansas, down in Harper and Barber counties, in flat and sandy areas that are dry most of the year. When the rains start each season, these small creatures make a memorable appearance, sometimes congregating by the thousands at choice sites, all the males calling and posturing as they await the arrival of the females. The females take their time about showing up at the watery ditches and low places and probably watch with amusement the antics of the males. But inevitably, the rite of renewal takes place, and young Strecker's Chorus Frogs abound in the wet sandy areas in a few weeks. Photograph by Suzanne L. Collins.

During the fall and winter months, flocks of Red-winged Blackbirds descend on Kansas fields and wetlands to consume large quantities of insects and seeds. Red-wings are usually the nucleus of these flocks, but Cowbirds, Grackles, and Starlings often manage to edge into the crowd. The red shoulder patch, called an epaulet, makes a male Red-winged Blackbird among the easiest of marsh birds to see and identify—particularly for the local raptors. The females are very different from the males, looking for all the world like large sparrows and blending well into a wetlands background. As far as they are concerned, the males can have the bright colors and sit singing on top of the grasses in full view. Let the hawks and snakes concentrate on Dad, while Mom stays hidden on the nest in the thick vegetation warming the eggs. Photograph by Bob Gress.

Chorusing Plains Leopard Frogs sound like the grating screech created when two balloons are rubbed together. When large numbers of these amphibians start to call simultaneously, it's a noise that can nettle the nerves. It's also a noise that attracts the attention of other nearby wetland residents, such as the Raccoon and Bullfrog. After a few nightly visits by these predators (and some frog-leg dinners), the Plains Leopard Frog population is more balanced and in tune with the surrounding wet meadows. Photograph by Suzanne L. Collins.

Biggest frog in Kansas, the Bullfrog makes good use of its size in many ways. A male Bullfrog is territorial and will alertly perch on the bank of an oxbow, jealously guarding its stretch of wetland shoreline. The largest male generally defends the most turf and gets the most food. Food includes anything it can catch, overpower, and swallow. At nightfall, young Bullfrogs are nervous and wary around the large frogs, because the big frogs are not very discriminating in their choice of dinner. Photograph by Suzanne L. Collins.

The Hooded Merganser is endemic to North America. Like the Wood Duck, this bird nests in tree cavities along riparian woodlands and frequents the temporary backwaters of forested floodplains. It breeds only occasionally in Kansas but is seen regularly during the winter months. This bird is a good diver and is an expert at capturing and holding onto fish with its serrated beak. During the spring courtship, males, like the one shown here, can be quite comical. Sometimes several drakes gather and follow after a female with their crests fully extended. Suitably excited, they next throw their heads way back and utter a strange, but nonetheless amorous, rolling "crrrroooo" followed by a hollow pop. The object of their affections, not to be outdone, responds with a romantic "gak," and together they swim off with idyllic low grunts and frog-like croaks. Photograph by Bob Gress.

A Killdeer nest can consist of little more than a shallow depression lined with small stones, but the speckled eggs within may be very difficult to see in the rocky surroundings. Pear-shaped eggs are typical of many birds that lay four per clutch, because they fit together nicely and are more easily covered by the relatively small incubating parent. Killdeer young are precocious, capable of running around shortly after hatching. Eggs of precocial birds are much larger and the incubation period longer than those of birds whose young are more helpless and undeveloped, or altricious. For example, a Killdeer and a Robin, which are about the same size, have very different chicks. The smaller Robin eggs hatch altricial young in only thirteen days, whereas the larger Killdeer eggs hatch precocial newborns in twenty-six days. Photograph by Bob Gress.

This plover is probably the most widely distributed and best known of all North American shorebirds. It is also quite proud of its name, constantly reminding us of it by calling "kill deer" whenever we are within hearing distance. Although it is often found near wetland environments, it is also at home in pastures and dry uplands miles from water. When feeding, the Killdeer runs rapidly across the ground and then stands still as if looking or listening. It often dips for an insect and then runs along to another spot to stop and look. When its nest or young are approached, the Killdeer is known for its "broken wing" display. In this way, many schoolchildren have been led away from the nest, which is often barely concealed in the gravel of their playground. The Killdeer is not known for its judicious selection of nesting sites. Photograph by David Birmingham.

Skilled anglers are often humbled by the fishing success of a Great Blue Heron. Equipped with quick reflexes, sharp eyes, and a beak that serves as a spear, this bird has just captured a fat Crappie for an evening snack, up in the shallow wetlands arm of Clinton Lake near Lawrence. Reservoirs proper are not wetlands, because their water is deep and permanent, but many do metamorphose into wetlands in their upper reaches, where the source of their water flows flat and shallow across thick mud, and anglers and fishes both have a difficult time maneuvering. Eventually, all the reservoirs in Kansas will become big lush wetlands, as silt from rainstorm runoff fills them up and turns them into broad mudflats. Great Blue Herons look forward to this evolution and will adapt well to the changing scene. We suspect anglers (and most fishes) will be uneasy at the prospect. Photograph by Bob Gress.

A verdant oxbow graces the floodplain of the Spring River in Cherokee County. These shallow backwaters are full of wildlife, from frogs and crayfishes to damselflies and ducks. An oxbow wetland often sports many kinds of fishes, but when the oxbow dries up barren and dormant, the fishes disappear. Like a true wetland, it awaits filling by the next downpour. If the nearby river overflows, too, a few fishes may return for another temporary visit, but their days are always numbered, at the mercy of rain, or lack of it. Photograph by Suzanne L. Collins.

Some fishes do well in wetlands, slipping in during the spring rainy season to look for food. Blackstripe Topminnows, like this one from a backwater in the South Fork of the Cottonwood River, Chase County, have a special reason for visiting wetlands—they love to eat mosquito larvae, and areas of still, trapped water are where these undesirable little insects breed. These little fishes have mouths that are situated high on the snout and are well adapted to feeding near the surface on wriggling mosquito larvae. With such an upward view of life, one might think they are subject to easy predation from below. Not so. When feeding, Topminnows reflect themselves in the water's undersurface and, when chased by a predator, they dart away at one angle while their mirror image goes in another. Such misdirection is effective in confusing a predator, and often allows the Topminnow to escape and continue to wreak havoc on mosquito populations. Photograph by Garold Sneegas.

Duckweed, floating on the surface of this Clay County marsh, can entirely cover a wetland surface in summer. Beneath the expanse of vivid green it is warm; algae thrives, thickening the still water to a rich broth. The moist soil in the roots of this fallen Cottonwood supports a small island of luxuriant plant life. To a frog, this dense swampy scene is nirvana. Photograph by Steve Mulligan.

The Dolomedes Spider is sometimes called the "fishing spider" because it lives around the ponds, ditches, and marshes of wetlands, where it easily skims along the surface of the water. When disturbed, this skittish invertebrate dives beneath the surface, breathing air that it traps in little bubbles on its hairy body. Although it mainly feeds on insects, this spider will also eat small tadpoles and fishes. In a wetlands marsh, most animals survive by feeding on other animals. The populations of different species can vary greatly from one year to the next. In years when the Bullfrog population is high, Dolomedes Spiders are a little jittery and eventually become scarce. Photograph by Bob Gress.

The Water Strider is a common sight, stepping out on the surface of all still or slow-moving bodies of water. Wetlands abound with this skittish little creature, and contrary to popular belief, Water Striders do not bite people. They do, however, glide swiftly across the surface of a watery roadside ditch and catch any small insects that have fallen into the drink. After catching them, they suck them dry of all nutritional juices. Photograph by Bob Gress.

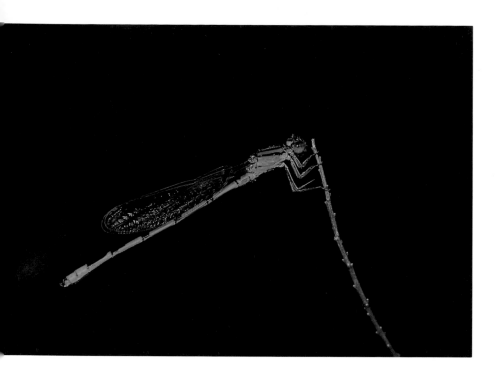

To many anglers, the Bluet is the only available wildlife action as it flutters about, landing and taking off from their bobber. From such a convenient hunting perch, the Bluet sallies forth to catch other, smaller insects, using its legs like a tiny basket to scoop them up on the wing. The Bluet prefers bright bare sunny areas along a wetland shoreline. Although two distinct groups, damselflies and dragonflies are closely related. Combined there are about three hundred kinds of them in North America. The Bluet is a damselfly and differs from a dragonfly by having a much thinner, more delicate body and wings that fold over the back. Photograph by Bob Gress.

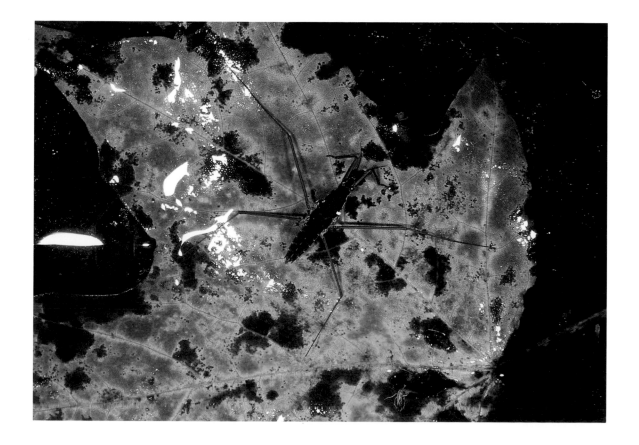

The life history of the Giant Water Bug could form the basis of an entomological "monster" movie. These two-and-a-half-inch aquatic predators use their powerful front legs to capture some surprisingly large prey, including tadpoles, small frogs, salamanders, and even small fishes. While holding their prey they puncture it with their stout sucking beak, inject it with poisonous saliva, then suck out the liquid parts. Although the Giant Water Bug is normally found in the water, it is also a good flier and is sometimes attracted to street lamps. Because of this fascination with lamps, it is sometimes called the electric light bug. Another common name is "toe-biter." Guess how it got that name. Photograph by Bob Gress.

During spring months, vast hordes of adult Mayflies are sometimes encountered in or near the wetlands of our state. When disturbed they swarm into the air, then settle back down, sometimes landing all over the arms, legs, and faces of nearby folks. To the unsuspecting, this often creates sheer panic with lots of running, swatting, and screaming. The insects are actually quite harmless and frail. They cannot bite and live only a day or two, long enough to breed and lay their eggs in the water. After hatching, the larvae live two or three years before emerging during some future spring to excite a new crop of wetland visitors. Photograph by Bob Gress.

Stumps and dead trees standing like ancient sentinels are typical of the shallow wetlands at Marais des Cygnes Wildlife Area. Wood Ducks, Prothonotary Warblers, Double-crested Cormorants, and migrating Ospreys are commonly seen here, and aquatic turtles and snakes love to sit on the stumps and bask in the sun. Trees that grow on floodplains face an uncertain future; if their roots are covered by floodwaters for too long a time, they will die. After a period of no flooding, of course, new trees sprout and the cycle begins anew. But the odds favor the wetlands, because flooding most surely will occur again. Photograph by Bob Gress.

Scattered across central and western Kansas are shallow depressions in the land called playas. During years of good rainfall, these basins fill and become large shallow wetlands, displacing the croplands that more and more frequently cover these lowlands. If the rainfall persists, wetland plants sometimes appear, such as Cattails, Spike Sedge, Plains Coreopsis, and Dock. Many kinds of wildlife benefit from these shallow catch-basins, surviving around them until the concavities are again transformed into vital wetlands. Photograph by Bob Gress.

To people who hate swatting mosquitoes, the Green Darner is a welcome sight. This insect is the largest and the fastest dragonfly in Kansas. With a wingspread of four inches, the adults chase not only mosquitoes, but also midges and caddisflies. They catch a lot of them and consume them with gusto. Like other dragonflies, when at rest this creature holds its wings outstretched. The colorful Green Darner has a greenish thorax and a bluish abdomen. Photograph by Gerald J. Wiens.

Arrowhead gets its name from the shape of its leaves. On the rootlike rhizome, buried in the mud, is a starch-filled tuber that has been used by many Native American tribes of North America as an important food source, usually boiled or roasted. In 1805, members of the Lewis and Clark Expedition were introduced to Arrowhead by Native Americans, and the explorers considered it a good substitute for bread. Different parts of this plant are eaten by many different kinds of animals. Photograph by Bob Gress.

Cattails are common in marshes and ditches and in the shallow areas of ponds, lakes, and slow-moving streams. There are three kinds in Kansas, and they reach new areas by means of their wind-blown seeds. They sometimes form vast colonies, growing to heights of nearly eight feet, with leaves so densely packed that they create a solid curtain of vegetation. Hidden in the Cattails are a variety of frogs and turtles and an abundance of birds like Coots, Rails, and Bitterns. Red-winged Blackbirds nest in the plants, and Muskrats like to eat their roots and rhizomes. Some Cattails are beneficial, but some large marshes, like Cheyenne Bottoms, have so many Cattails that they create a problem. Other plants that provide food and cover to wildlife are sometimes crowded out. Photograph by Bob Gress.

After a day spent searching for frogs, fishes, crayfishes, and insects, Egrets skim over a marsh on the way to their evening roost. Kansas wetlands are important, not only to wildlife, but to people as well. Wetlands and their aquatic plants assist in filtering pollutants and toxins and help control flooding by catching excess water from rainstorms. While holding that water, they also replenish the ground-water in the area. To outdoor enthusiasts, wetlands provide great opportunities to birdwatch during the day, hunt snakes and frogs by night, and watch Egrets at sunset. Photograph by Bob Gress.

Wetlands were once considered dangerous, forbidding places. They were dubbed wastelands, full of useless snakes, turtles, frogs, and birds. Mosquitoes and other biting insects swarmed naturally in these low places, and those who ventured into them after dark gave blood the old-fashioned way—against their will. Today, visitors are better prepared with repellents and wildlife field guides. Armed with binoculars and cameras, they quickly discover the rich rewards to be had by slopping around in these moist environments. They still get bitten by mosquitoes, but no pain, no gain. Photograph by Bob Gress.

Prairie Cordgrass is sometimes called "sloughgrass" or "marshgrass." It usually grows in lowland areas that are prone to seasonal flooding and drying. Early Kansas pioneers used this plant for thatching roofs and quickly learned that the grass blades are tough. The teeth on the margins of each blade can deliver a nasty cut, and many a settler probably created one or two new English word combinations while harvesting it. The grass does, however, make good hay if cut while young and tender. In this photograph, a Least Bittern pauses in Prairie Cordgrass while hunting for minnows. Photograph by Bob Gress.

With a name like Smartweed you'd think it would be popular on tossed salads in school cafeterias. Unfortunately it doesn't work. (The authors have tried it.) These plants occur in wet fields, ditches, marshes, and pond edges, and their seeds are relished by the waterfowl and many other birds that frequent such wetlands. The flowers of Smartweed range in color from pale pink to bright red. When in bloom, they attract lots of flies, honeybees, wasps, and even moths. The presence of so many insects lures a lot of frogs to the area. The abundance of frogs guarantees that water snakes will make an appearance. And they all run for safety when the egrets and herons show up. Photograph by Bob Gress.

Suggested Reading

Bare, Janét. 1979. *Wildflowers and Weeds of Kansas.* University Press of Kansas (Lawrence). 509 pp.

Barkley, Theodore M. 1983. *Field Guide to the Common Weeds of Kansas.* University Press of Kansas (Lawrence). 164 pp.

Bee, James W., Gregory E. Glass, Robert S. Hoffmann, and Robert R. Patterson. 1981. *Mammals in Kansas.* University of Kansas Museum of Natural History Public Education Series No. 7. 300 pp.

Borrer, Donald J., and Richard E. White. 1970. *A Field Guide to Insects of America North of Mexico.* Peterson Field Guide No. 19. Houghton Mifflin (Boston). 404 pp.

Burt, William Henry. 1976. *A Field Guide to the Mammals of North America North of Mexico.* 3d ed. Peterson Field Guide No. 5. Houghton Mifflin (Boston). 289 pp.

Collins, Joseph T. 1993. *Amphibians and Reptiles in Kansas.* 3d ed. University of Kansas Museum of Natural History Public Education Series No. 13. 397 pp.

Collins, Joseph T., and Suzanne L. Collins. 1993. *Reptiles and Amphibians of Cheyenne Bottoms.* Hearth Publishing (Hillsboro, Kans.). 92 pp.

Collins, Joseph T., Bob Gress, Gerald J. Wiens, and Suzanne L. Collins. 1991. *Kansas Wildlife.* University Press of Kansas (Lawrence). 127 pp.

Conant, Roger, and Joseph T. Collins. 1991. *A Field Guide to the Reptiles and Amphibians of Eastern and Central North America.* 3d ed. Peterson Field Guide No. 12. Houghton Mifflin (Boston). 608 pp.

Cowardin, Lewis M., Virginia Carter, Francis C. Golet, and Edward T. LaRoe. 1979. *Classification of Wetlands and Deepwater Habitats of the United States.* U.S. Department of the Interior Fish and Wildlife Service Publication (Washington, D.C.). 131 pp.

Cross, Frank B., and Joseph T. Collins. 1975. *Fishes in Kansas.* University of Kansas Museum of Natural History Public Education Series No. 5. 189 pp.

Galatowitsch, Susan M., and Arnold G. van der Valk. 1994. *Restoring Prairie Wetlands: An Ecological Approach.* Iowa State University Press (Ames). 344 pp.

Gress, Bob, and George Potts. 1993. *Watching Kansas Wildlife. A Guide to 101 Sites.* University Press of Kansas (Lawrence). 104 pp.

Murie, Olaus J. 1974. *Animal Tracks.* 2d ed. Peterson Field Guide No. 9. Houghton Mifflin (Boston). 375 pp.

Niering, William A. 1985. *Wetlands.* A. A. Knopf (New York). 638 pp.

Page, Lawrence M., and Brooks M. Burr. 1991. *A Field Guide to the Freshwater Fishes of North America North of Mexico.* Peterson Field Guide No. 42. Houghton Mifflin (Boston). 544 pp.

Peterson, Roger Tory. 1980. *A Field Guide to the Birds of Eastern and Central North America.* 4th ed. Peterson Field Guide No. 1. Houghton Mifflin (Boston). 384 pp.

Stephens, H. A. 1969. *Trees, Shrubs, and Woody Vines in Kansas.* University Press of Kansas (Lawrence). 250 pp.

Thompson, Max C., and Charles Ely. 1989. *Birds in Kansas.* Vol. 1. University of Kansas Museum of Natural History Public Education Series No. 11. 404 pp.

Thompson, Max C., and Charles Ely. 1992. *Birds in Kansas.* Vol. 2. University of Kansas Museum of Natural History Public Education Series No. 12. 424 pp.

Weller, Milton W. 1994. *Freshwater Marshes: Ecology and Wildlife Management.* 3d ed. University of Minnesota Press (Minneapolis). 192 pp.

Williams, D. Dudley. 1987. *The Ecology of Temporary Waters.* Timber Press (Portland, Ore.). 205 pp.

Zimmerman, John L. 1990. *Cheyenne Bottoms. Wetland in Jeopardy.* University Press of Kansas (Lawrence). 197 pp.

Index